In this series –

RUMI READINGS
FOR
LOVE

RUMI READINGS
FOR
LOVE

JALALUDDIN RUMI

The Scheherezade Foundation

The Scheherazade Foundation CIC
85 Great Portland Street
London
W1W 7LT
United Kingdom
www.SF.Charity
info@SF.Charity

First published by The Scheherazade Foundation CIC, 2025

RUMI READINGS FOR LOVE

© The Scheherazade Foundation

A CIP catalogue record for this title is available from the British Library.

ISBN 978-1-915311-74-0

Introduction

Jalaluddin Rumi was born in Balkh, Afghanistan, in the year 1207, and died in Konya, Turkey, in 1273.

During the sixty-six years spanning this pair of dates, he produced a range of extraordinary work in Persian which, today, is classed as 'Sufi Mysticism'.

In the seven and a half centuries since his death, Rumi's corpus, which includes *The Masnavi* and *Fihi Ma Fihi*, has been circulated widely across the Near East, the Arab world, and Central Asia.

Generations of students continue to commit selections of the 60,000 verses to heart, and allow Rumi's way of thought to permeate through all areas of their lives.

Although Orientalists venturing eastward from Europe in the 1700s occasionally made note of Sufi Mysticism, they tended to witness it through the more theatrical frills – such as 'whirling dervishes' – rather than through a deep appreciation of the texts.

It wasn't until the close of the nineteenth century that the first wholescale translations of Rumi's written work began to appear in Europe.

Even then, they remained very much the purview of a few academics, whose translations were – even for the time – laden with indescribably floral and cumbersome prose.

Although in the Occident, students would find themselves scrutinizing Rumi's corpus, it wasn't until more recently that accessible appreciations of his work became available.

A few years before his death, I asked my father – the Sufi scholar and thinker Idries Shah – for his thoughts on Rumi's legacy in the West.

Sitting in his favourite chair, a porcelain cup of green tea in hand, he looked at me hard.

'I never cease to be amazed,' he said.

'Amazed by what?'

'By the way people don't take what's perfectly packaged, and ready and waiting for them, but rather obsess with something else.'

'With what?'

'With endless and nonsensical trimmings, trappings, and paraphernalia.'

My father sipped his tea.

After a moment of silent thought, he continued:

'Read Rumi in the original Persian,' he said, 'and so delicate are the verses that you have tears rolling down your cheeks. Yet here in the West, it's served up as something submerged in a thick, glutinous gravy, so much so that its utterly inedible.'

I reminded my father that a series of publications had recently found their way to press – publications that presented Rumi's couplets in an utterly new way.

Stripped bare of what my father had referred to as 'gravy', they were light.

Indeed, they were lighter than light.

My father rolled his eyes at the thought.

'In any other place, and at any other time,' he said, 'people would be up in arms. Or, if they weren't, they'd be laughing until their sides split. Imagine it – Western poets with absolutely no knowledge of the original Persian text touting new, bestselling editions of Rumi's work! It's what we call "The Soup of the Soup of the Soup".'

In the years since my father's death, Occidental society has been flooded with all things Rumi.

Couplets ascribed to him are read solemnly at weddings across the United States, Europe, and beyond.

Wisdom drawn from his poetry is tattooed daily over the backs and limbs of Hollywood A-listers.

But the precious words uttered at weddings, tattooed into skin, and quoted in abundance, hold little or no bearing to the original verses of Jalaluddin Rumi.

So, there it is…

The great Sufi Master's wisdom available:

(a) in a form that's unreadable because it's all covered in glutinous gravy, or

(b) in another form that's completely distorted – the Soup of the Soup of the Soup.

One thing that *is* evident is that the West can benefit enormously from a clean, clear rendition of Rumi's thinking – as the East has done over the last seven hundred years.

For this reason, we have commissioned entirely new translations, gleaned in particular from *The Masnavi*. Selected and translated by native Persian-speaking scholars, the emphasis has been on maintaining the lightness of Rumi's poetry.

In an age of relentless speed and digital overload, and so as to allow the work to be accessed by those who may benefit from it most, we have arranged a series of bite-sized morsels by way of theme.

We encourage you to do what students, scholars, and ordinary people have done across the East for centuries...

To pick a single couplet, or a handful – and to read them over and over, allowing them to seed themselves in your mind.

Little by little, having taken root, they will blossom and bear fruit.

Tahir Shah

How to Use This Book

Rumi Readings for Love

This book is for lovers.

For those who are in love, and for those who have been broken by it.

For those who long, who burn, who tremble, who remember.

And for those who wonder if what they feel is love at all.

It is also for those who have discovered something deeper...

A love that transcends one person, one moment, one form...

The kind of love that unravels the self and stitches it back together as something truer.

Rumi Readings for Love gathers one hundred selections from the original Persian poetry of Jalaluddin Rumi, translated faithfully by The Scheherazade Foundation. These quotes are drawn especially from *The Masnavi* and arranged into ten thematic parts, exploring love as longing, as union, as fire, as paradox – and above all, as a path toward transformation.

This is not a book of sentiment. It is not here to romanticize or simplify.

It is a book of mirrors – and flames.

Let it show you who you are when you are loving, when you are losing, when you are opening, and when you are being opened.

Love Is Not One Thing

Love is not only sweetness.

It is also pain, contradiction, laughter, silence, surrender, and power.

It moves through stages. It sheds skins. It changes the names on its lips.

This book is not meant to define love – only to reflect it as it moves through you.

Let each quote meet you where you are.

Let it echo what you need, or disturb what you thought you knew.

Sometimes, one line will say more than a lifetime of explanations.

Other times, you may feel nothing. That's fine.

Keep returning. Love is always returning.

Read One Quote at a Time

You do not need to read this all at once.
   You may not want to.

   Try reading one quote at a time. Let it speak, and then
be silent.

   You may want to sit with it for an hour. Or a week.
   You may write it down. Whisper it. Memorize it. Leave it
under someone's pillow.
   Or you may simply breathe it in, like a scent you can't
name but cannot forget.

   This is how love works.

A Practice of Reflection

After reading a quote, ask yourself:

- What kind of love is this pointing to?
- Where have I seen this in my own life – or longed to?
- What does this quote stir in me – desire, resistance, grief, clarity?

You can let the question hang unanswered.

If your heart is full – or aching – that space can be a quiet place to pour what words cannot hold.

Love in Solitude, Love in Union

You may be reading this book alone. Or with someone you love. Or after losing someone. Or while searching.

There is no wrong moment to engage with love.

Rumi reminds us again and again: what looks like absence may be presence. What looks like heartbreak may be invitation.

Let the quotes remind you that you are not separate from love.
Even when it feels distant. Even when it disappears.

Let them bring you back to the source.

Share Them

You may find a quote that speaks for you – better than you could speak for yourself.

Send it. Read it aloud. Use it as a vow, a question, a blessing.

Give it without explanation. Receive it without needing to understand.

This is love's language. It goes beyond logic.

Let the Fire Do Its Work

Not every quote will comfort you.
Some will burn.

Rumi does not flinch from the wildness of love. He tells us plainly: love may undo you.

But he also shows that this undoing is sacred. It makes space for something real to enter.

Let the fire burn what is false. Let it soften what is rigid.
Let it teach you how to remain open, even when it hurts.

Rumi writes in this volume:
'Love carries its own keys, ready to unlock any closed door or challenges in its way.'

So let the door open.
Let the threshold become your altar.
And let these words walk beside you – in every stage, in every form, in every echo of love.

Part 1

Discovering
the Duties of Love

1

Whatever words a lover utters,
the fragrance of that love spreads forth from their lips
with every step of the path they tread.

2

When love is ignited,
it becomes a blazing flame
that consumes everything
except the object of affection:
the beloved.

3

The paradox is this:
the beloved encompasses both unity
and your own existence.
Within the beloved lie both beginning and end.
Once found, all waiting dissolves,
for it is both revealed and concealed,
a hidden knowledge.

4

Your cruelty surpasses any riches,
and your revenge is more precious
than the life of the beloved.
Tell me, how brightly does your passion burn?
And how long must I mourn
until I find solace in you?

5

Do not taunt me with the threat of death,
for my heart is open to the ecstasy your blow may bring.
For the lover, death is an ever-present companion;
there are myriad ways to sacrifice for love.
Each breath is a reminder of boundless devotion,
a willingness to give up two hundred lives
in the name of sacrifice.

6

To be truly generous,
there must be no hesitation to give every last coin.
For a lover's ultimate act of generosity
is to lay down their own life.

7

With passion's fire ablaze,
the lover fervently declared their quest for the beloved.
But upon the beloved's arrival,
the lover's very existence was extinguished.

8

True lovers traverse both joy and sorrow
within the realm of their beloved,
discovering their reward and satisfaction in serving them.
Anything but the gaze of their beloved holds no meaning,
for it is not love,
but aimless pursuit.

9

With you, they say, these mountains are steadfast,
describing the state of lovers in stability.

10

Embrace the diversity within you.
Shapeshift like the sun and the sea.
Be a towering mountain, a magnificent phoenix,
yet never confined by one form, one label.
Transcend all illusion and extravagance within,
beyond comparison, beyond limitation.

Part 2

The State & Manners
of the Beloved

.

11

A true lover is driven by the desire for unity,
not by motives of self.
It is not the lover who pursues
but the beloved who draws them near.
Like a bolt of lightning, love ignites within this heart.
But in the heart of a friend, its presence is revealed.

12

The beloved's yearning is elusive and delicate,
while the lover's longing is proclaimed with grand parade.
The all-encompassing love shared between
true lovers may give way to physical decline,
yet the love reciprocated by the beloved
brings only joy and vitality to being.

13

Love is like a loyal companion:
it buys devotion,
and pays no attention to a disloyal adversary.

14

The melding of hearts should constantly evolve,
like the ever-changing moon in its journey across the sky.
For those in distress, this love is the cure.
Let us not worsen their pain,
but hasten its obscurity.
No panacea is as potent as this poisoned bliss.
From this sickness, no cure is more pure and holy.

15

When it comes to love, exercise caution
and refrain from cultivating admirers.
Playing with the affections of two lovers
is a perilous game.

16

The lovers, swept away by a swift current,
have surrendered to the unpredictable voyage of love.
As if caught by the planet's gravitational pull,
they whirl endlessly, consumed by their yearning and sorrow,
unable to escape the relentless cycle.

17

Gaze upon the beloved ceaselessly,
for they lie within your grasp.
Discover your inner compass,
and banish all emptiness.

18

A beautiful quince, its skin
a vibrant blend of red and yellow,
whispered a tale of passion and zest.
As the lover and the beloved faced separation,
the beloved adorned themselves with flirtation,
while the lover bore the burden of heartache.
Yet even in their separation,
these contrasting hues reflected
a mutual love in their respective expressions.
The beloved's delicate complexion
shied away from the warmth of yellow,
while the lover's rosy plumage emitted
a coolness that betrayed their inner turmoil.

19

'Don't bother me. Go away!'
Your flirtatious remark
sparks a yearning within me
for even more heartache.
And it is my deepest desire
to fulfil your request.

20

Love begets unique identities
when two souls stand apart;
the intangible finds manifestation in their union.
I embody both wisdom and passion;
our reflection is shaped
by the beauty we perceive.
I have dismantled the barriers,
laid bare the authentic essence of beauty.
In the moment of our reunion
the imperceptible adopts a palpable form.

Part 3
The Role of Love

21

Love possesses the alchemical power
to transmute bitterness into sweetness,
turning copper into gold with its gentle touch.
Even the most undesirable remnants are purified by love,
and our greatest pains are cured by its healing embrace.

22

Within the turmoil of separation lies anger;
but recognizing the true importance of their bond is crucial.
Only by giving in to the pain of parting,
does the soul grasp the true value of reunion.

23

Anyone whose clothing was torn by love
found themselves freed from desire or wrongdoing.
Love, you are a source of joy,
our sweet cure and the healer of all our afflictions.

24

The belt symbolizes the captivating allure of love.
For who, other than the wearer,
could resist its tempting embrace?

25

A majestic bird perches upon your crown;
its fluttering feathers stirring your very essence.
Remain still, for any sudden movement may startle it;
causing your vibrant bird to take flight.
Whether uttering sweetness or bitterness,
a finger to your lips commands silence.
The marvel of this bird is to still you,
as though placing upon your head a pot of steaming water,
at once both scalding and cooling.

26

While your mind races with
a hundred pressing thoughts,
surrounded by myriad desires, fears and hopes,
unite these scattered pieces
with the embrace of love.
Blossom into a wondrous tapestry,
like Samarkand,
like Paradise.

27

Everlasting love sustains us,
even in death;
our hearts and souls tethered,
imbued with life-giving breath.
Your boundless affection
flows within our reach:
a miraculous elixir,
nourishing us with every gasp.

28

Without a beloved,
the heart feels incomplete,
like a person without a mind.
And those who steer clear of love's temptation
are like birds without the freedom to fly.

29

Take hold of the reins of love
and embrace the journey,
for the steed of love is without a rider.
In one swift stride
it will carry you to your desired end,
no matter the challenges and obstacles along the way.

30

Love carries its own keys,
ready to unlock any closed door
or challenges in its way.

Part 4
The Role of Reason in Love

31

Though love may appear to conceal secrets,
its true nature is elusive.
It can deceive with cunning wisdom,
yet it cannot truly be deemed an angel
until it transforms into one.
In both words and actions of love,
trust is elusive
as it may not stand with us in times of Judgement.

32

Have you ever wondered what love truly is?
It is like being submerged
in an endless sea
where logic and reason cease to exist.
If you dare dive in,
be prepared to have your entire world
turned upside down.

33

Dear soul,
let love win the debate,
for it becomes the advocate in our dialogue.
Marvel at the words of love;
it is not the planet Venus that shares this story.

34

At every single instant
our hearts are fuelled
by a unique desire.
With every sigh
we ignite a fresh spark of passion within.
The compass of judgement now
points solely to the heart.
We prioritize the heart above all else,
recognizing superficiality as nothing
but fleeting elements of water and clay.

35

Your reasoning is admirable,
O accused one,
but how can I solidify and give value to something
that has turned into dust?
We must bring together the components
under the direction of love
so that it may shine with the same beauty
as Samarkand and Damascus.

36

In the pursuit of love, one must let go of reason,
for love cannot thrive beside logic.
Instead, seek the wisdom that stems
from the very core of that love,
for it is the foundation that guides its every aspect.

37

Love surpasses thought, because thought is weak.
My reason rebels, leaving me blind.

38

We were consumed with desire to savour Layla's wine.
Dear love!
You are the great enemy of logic and sense.
And logic, you were once mere copper,
but in the presence of love
you became precious gold.
Now you surpass alchemy itself,
embodying the very essence and understanding of alchemy.

39

At what point does reason succumb to despair?
Love, undaunted by obstacles, soars above the haze.
Unlike reason, which strives for personal gain,
love seeks no profit, its eyes set on higher purpose.

40

Good people courageously chased after their goals,
yet they found only defeat and were unable to succeed.
And in the aftermath of their setbacks,
what became of them?
And what happened to the lovers
when their hearts were broken?
Despite their honesty and determination,
those people faced challenges brought on by greater forces,
that hindered their aspirations.
But those consumed by love
went on to fulfil their desires with passion
and determination.
While the wise were driven by obligation
in their pursuit of truth,
the lovers willingly surrendered to their desires
with happy hearts and unwavering devotion.

Part 5

What Love Causes

41

Embrace your restlessness
as a means of seeking my presence.
Allow yourself to become a lover brimming with energy,
and let tranquility find you in the process.

42

The desire for companionship is inherent in matter,
allowing for mutual effort to lead to fulfilment.
God has ordained this longing in you,
sustaining the world through unity
of complementary forces.

43

Cling to his robe with unwavering certainty
to discover the path towards the end of times.
The guidebook and sacred portraits by our side
serve as proof of God's illuminating light.

44

The once bitter taste transforms into sweet nectar,
gently caressing your lips.
Thorns, once perceived as threats,
radiate beauty in the midst of the rose garden.
The promises of the beloved,
with a face as radiant as the moon,
have enticed many a would-be lover
to remove any thorns in their path.
Heavy burdens are easily carried by their bearers,
all for the affection of the beloved.

45

As two become one,
you embody that unity.
As individuality fades,
you are what remains.
The merging of 'you' and 'me' creates one soul,
ultimately merging with the divine.

46

Love is the solace that eases difficulties,
a balm that soothes the anguish of the desolate.
Through trials and tribulations
love is the remedy for human suffering.
Love transforms thorns into blooming flowers,
and tears down walls to build bridges.

47

Love is the essential ingredient
for a bountiful harvest of joy and delight.
Without this deep connection
life lacks goodness and harmony.
No amount of worldly pleasures,
like drops of rain in a vast sea, can act as substitute
for the transformative power of love.
It is what imbues the unseen and intangible
with sweetness and meaning.

48

In this journey of life
many people come and go,
contributing to its beginning
but failing to witness its end.
The absence of you weighs heavily on my heart;
no other presence can fill the void you leave behind.
Despite logic's deceptive allure,
the unyielding grip of destiny,
and the tantalizing promise of happiness,
they all pale in comparison
without your presence to complete them.

49

When the world is filled with thorns,
the heart of the lover blossoms like a garden of flowers.
Even when the skies darken,
the realm of lovers remains vibrant
and teeming with life. Amidst the sorrows of others,
the lover's spirit remains gentle, joyful, and discerning.

50

Love resembles an infinite ocean,
granting the boon of everlasting existence
to unfortunate souls.

Part 6

Choosing a
Suitable Companion

51

Amidst this serenity,
I am intrigued to discover,
who is deserving of a woman as remarkable as you?
Allow me to declare
that you have not only become my companion,
but a person of humility and integrity in my eyes.

52

Love that lacks depth and authenticity is never true;
it ends in disgrace.

53

Captivated by allure and physical charm,
the body moved gracefully
while the soul stayed concealed,
adorned with elegance and delicate wings.
Curiously, the soul questioned the passing entity:
'O transient one, reveal yourself.
For a fleeting moment,
you basked in my radiant light.'

54

To create harmony in relations,
compatibility with the beloved is essential.
Just as with a pair of shoes,
the right fit is key:
when one shoe is too tight or too loose,
the two cannot work as a pair.
Even in an environment of harmony,
mismatched individuals cannot coexist in peace.

55

Do not be swayed solely
by superficial appearance in matters of love.
While external beauty may catch the eye,
true love seeks to explore the deeper essence
and inner beauty of the beloved.

56

I hold a secret within myself
that is shared only with you;
beyond this, there is no
shortage of captivating faces in the world.

57

If you long for gratitude,
then see her through the adoring eyes
of her loyal admirers. Set aside your own view,
and instead gaze at the beloved
through the eyes of those who seek her.

58

Love and beauty intertwine,
each enhancing the other.
While beauty alone does not guarantee love,
being loved is integral to true beauty.
When someone is deeply loved,
their beauty shines forth.
The essence of being loved encompasses true beauty;
the two are inseparable.
Beauty should not be seen in isolation,
but as part of the whole.

59

A human being is a unique creation,
endowed with great knowledge and wisdom.
This inner truth cannot be concealed,
but the distractions of the world,
deceit and desires,
act as a veil, casting shadows,
blocking our path to this inner knowing.

60

Your physical presence bears witness
to the journey of the soul,
for the Prophet has declared:
'Blessed is the act of witnessing.'
The earthly form that veils us is transient,
but the grace bestowed upon us from
above is truly blessed.

Part 7

The Etiquette of Union

61

There was a gentleman with a beautiful daughter,

exuding elegance and charm.

Her hand was sought by princes,

each vying for her attentions and affection.

But the father cautioned,

'Wealth is fickle and unstable;

It can quickly come and quickly go.

And beauty, though alluring, holds no true merit;

It can easily fade with the prick of a thorn.

A prince may easily be deceived by wealth and status.

The true keys to success and prosperity lie

in devotion and virtue,

as through them alone come blessings to the world.'

62

As each particle adoringly joins its beloved,
they stand together,
ready to bond and be united.
In this sacred union
water and fire have intertwined,
giving birth to the hyacinth
and the lily.

63

Let us rejoice in this blessed union;
may it bring us unending joy.
With a good repute,
shining beauty, and abundant blessings,
our love glimmers like the moon and the emerald sky.
Let us celebrate this union
with gratitude,
with happiness.

64

When you stray from His light,
you become a mere wanderer,
all purpose lost.
Let us hold tight to this ring
as a symbol, a reminder,
to stay true to our commitment.

65

As I fastened the belt,
joy overflowed in my heart.
I could not help but unveil the face of the moon,
trapped by its all-absorbing beauty.

66

The lover's gifts are fleeting,
for they come from mere wealth and fortune,
always finding a way back to their beginnings.
Although the groom may receive great riches from the
beloved, His own wealth and dowry
go no further than the grave.

67

To express his joy and celebrate their reunion,
the lover decorates the surroundings
to enchant the beloved's heart,
making this day unique among all others.

68

The world becomes like a wedding within the soul,
mirroring the radiance of the bride's countenance,
like those of two newly married women,
decorated and vivified.

69

For those who have not witnessed the depths
of their own heart,
for those whose eyes cannot catch the glimmer of their moon,
what purpose do music and drums serve?
For music is meant to reunite us with the one we hold dear.

70

Let us raise a glass to the lady who,
on this joyous occasion, becomes the bride,
and to the man who,
swept away by the currents of your love,
ascends to new heights,
and takes on the title of 'groom'.

Part 8

The Importance of Women in Building a Meaningful Partnership

71

Whatever actions you take with her,
O trusted one,
may God mirror your actions,
whether good or bad.

72

Her glow emanates from Truth,
not from love;
it belongs to the Creator,
not the created being.

73

According to the Prophet,
women have the upper hand over the wise
and the learned.
History repeats itself as women surpass men
lacking in knowledge.
This is due to the inherent quickness
that lies in a woman's nature,
like the agility of an untamed animal.

74

Just as water can overcome fire,
so too can man dominate woman.
But woman has the ability
to spark fire and control it,
like a vessel or pot acts
as mediator between water and fire.

75

As the lady of the soul,
she made her home in the mansion of the body.
With a mystic veil adorning her,
she embarked on a new journey of love.

76

Passion is the cherished elixir that endures,
for it pours forth the invigorating
nectar of your very being.

77

Listen to her with an open mind,
and embrace her guidance,
even if it challenges your beliefs.
Let go of jealousy,
whether directed towards other men or towards yourself.
Remember, both positive and negative descriptions
stem from the same source.

78

Have you ever seen a Majnun
who yearned for two Laylas,[1]
unable to choose between them?
Direct your heart toward one,
rather than being torn between false choices.

---

1   A reference to the classic Middle Eastern love story of Layla and Majnun.

79

The soul may be feminine,
but is neither timid nor reserved,
and not defined by gender.
It does not see 'male' or 'female'.
The soul's essence does not depend on
people's ideas of dryness or wetness.

80

The sky is man and the earth is woman in wisdom.
Whatever the man sows, the woman nurtures.

Part 9
Managing Love

81

Their profound belief in fate and destiny
has ignited a passionate love between us.
Nature's elements are intricately intertwined by this force,
bringing lovers together in perfect harmony.
A universal yearning for connection leads
every entity to its destined match,
just as amber is drawn to straw in true union.

82

Speaking with an angered man
can lead to distress and hostility.
Confronted with unexpected treatment,
'love' can swiftly become frustration and bitterness.

83

As his harsh and angry gaze falls upon her,
tears freely flow down her face, ensnaring her.
My entire being,
every inch and every breath, belongs to you;
your every wish and word hold sway, it is true.

84

As the rain poured down,
a lightning bolt struck
straight into the heart of the lonely man.
With tears in his eyes,
he cried out to the woman before him,
'I beg forgiveness, for if I have wronged.
I vow to embrace faith.
I am but a sinner,
begging for your mercy.
Please, do not cast me out to eternal emptiness.'

85

Your words were inspired and insightful,
but I would like to discuss this first with a trusted friend.

86

No amount of status or popularity can replace
the need for a confidant,
someone to whom one you can open your heart
and share deepest secrets.

87

As you walk along the high wall,
beware, for its uneven edges may deceive.
And in an instant, my beloved, intoxicated by worry,
emerged, clutching her cloak in haste.
Furious with the fickle love of this woman,
I cried out, 'Do you see my heartache?'
Yet she did not ask, nor attempt to hide.

88

On being accused by him,
our relationship darkens.
A cloud hangs over me,
luring me towards a sorrow that was never his.
If I speak out
he weaves a web of lies, and paints
his wife as unfaithful,
forcefully driving me away,
and using tricks
to justify his wrongdoing.

89

Relationships have a deeper purpose than merely
to satisfy desires.
Our unique identities are not fleeting, like the air.
Our souls are like chess pieces,
carefully placed in God's hand.
With these pieces
we engage in a dance with those around us,
like a foolish flirt and her suitors.
But this game is not driven by superficial love
or fleeting passions.
It is a lesson for us to teach and learn from each other.
How long will our struggles and battles
in relationships continue?

90

Why do you seek a companion if you have none?
And why not rejoice if you have already found one?
Why not become a companion yourself
if you cannot find one in someone else?
If the lute refuses to sing,
why not teach it and guide its strings?
Sitting idle, is this not a wonder to see?
For you, my friend,
are the possessor of such wondrous passion.

Part 10

Secrets of Longevity or Failure in Relationships

91

Layla declared to Majnun,
'You have the title of caliph,
for it was your love that made me mad,
bewildered, and adrift.
Among all the beauties in the world,
None can compare to you.'
In response, he admonished her:
'Hush now, for you are not Majnun.
If jealousy threatens to consume you,
even the devil himself would struggle
to maintain his composure.'

92

As you imbibe the intoxicating love that floods
your soul, and become one with your beloved,
your identity fades into nothing.
Your very being is intertwined with theirs,
creating a bond in which any pain
or hardship you experience also touches them.
It is of utmost importance now to shield yourself from harm,
not just for your own sake,
but to safeguard the one you love.

93

Gazing upon the beloved,
the lover poured their heart out,
recounting every deed and sacrifice made –
wealth, power, reputation, all laid bare.
But their love still felt unfulfilled,
for there was something more essential at work.
The beloved spoke with wisdom,
'You have done much,
but true love is measured by what you forsake.'
The lover asked,
'What is this essence that eludes me?'
Solemnly, the beloved spoke:
'Love's true essence is death and nothingness.
Despite all you have given,
you have yet to die while still alive.
A true lover must be willing to embrace death
for their beloved,
for that is the ultimate sacrifice.'

94

One of the defining features of loving someone
is being able to remain indifferent,
even respond with anger,
when they express their love.
This challenge serves to gauge the sincerity
of their affection.
A wise lover, when confronted with this hostility,
will stand strong and resilient,
rather than succumb to distance
and endure the pain of separation.

95

Genuine love is when a devoted admirer discovers joy, splendour, and solace in the company of the beloved, with an unwavering faith that even the toughest trials become effortless and delightful with their presence.

96

As the lover handed the letter to his beloved,
he eagerly shared its contents aloud.
The words within were adorned with adoration
and sweet talk,
pleading for forgiveness and beseeching kindness.
In response, the beloved spoke,
'If this is all because of me,
then perhaps pursuing this union is a waste of time.'
The lover replied with heavy heart,
'Although I am here with you, I cannot find true joy.
What I beheld in you last year is not the same
in this moment of togetherness.'

97

The power of love knows no bounds,
reaching into the hearts of all.
Yet, only those who have prepared
and possess the right qualities
can fully embrace and reap the benefits of love.
Vigilance is the key to unlocking this world,
and those who lack it are better suited to find joy
elsewhere rather than attempting to enter into love
with half a heart.

98

As time passes and the radiance of his beauty fades,
the maiden's heart becomes entangled in its snare.
For when her once-fair face turns pallid and plain,
her heart grows cold and wretched.
Enmity, like the peacock's dazzling feathers,
can lead even the mightiest of rulers astray.
Like echoes bouncing off a mountainside,
our actions reverberate,
and hold us accountable in this world.

99

The tree before us has transformed into a mystical being,
its branches stretching towards the heavens above.
When you descend from its lofty height,
you are filled with a sense of detachment.
For in this moment our Creator
bestows upon us His mercy.
Through this humbling journey,
our eyes are opened to understanding and wisdom,
bestowed upon us by His grace.

100

The truth of marriage lies in the wisdom it holds,
born from necessity and the tumultuous
road once again, sought after for its worth.
But turn a blind eye and deafen your love's birth.

Finis

* 9 7 8 1 9 1 5 3 1 1 7 4 0 *